THE HARMONY
OF THE SPHERE

The Harmony of the Sphere

RAMUN BJERKEN

LUMINARE PRESS
WWW.LUMINAREPRESS.COM

The Harmony of the Sphere
Copyright © 2022 by Raymond Bjerken

All rights reserved. This book or any portion thereof may not be reproduced or used in any manner whatsoever without the express written permission of the publisher, except for the use of brief quotations in a book review.

Printed in the United States of America

Luminare Press
442 Charnelton St.
Eugene, OR 97401
www.luminarepress.com

LCCN: 2022904718
ISBN: 978-1-64388-951-1

This book is dedicated
to the two main inspiriations in my life,
my Mother, Mildred Prica Bjerken,
and Albert Einstein.

The book is also dedicated
to my immediate family:
Teva, Zeff, and Xak.

RAYMOND STEVEN BJERKEN
pen name, Ramun Bjerken
(1932–)

Contents

OR, An Alternative	1
Implications of OR	13
OR and the Axial Age	25
On My Poetry	29
My Introduction	33
A Possible Means	43

Poetry

The Hyphen	47
At a Mountain Meadow	51
Where goes the light	55
A Prequel to My Introduction	57
Stages	61
More Concerning My Poetry	67
A Triptych Night	69
Dragon	71
An Image for Reality	75
Boyhood Memories	77
Wolves	81
Seeking a Taoist Gate	85
Femininity	87

The Cave	89
A Quantum Function	91
Here is Where	93
Words Without Art	95
Cross-Country Skiing	97
Tree	99
Harness the Beast	101
Ageing	103

OR, An Alternative

Spirituality as an immediate experience has been realized as concrete by unique individuals since earliest history, but those special cases of direct personal participation could not meaningfully comunicate that experience without grasping some degree of its nature in intellect; its presence was often respected and rendered significant by religions through poetry and imagery. It eventually was labeled the "mystic experience". This property also has a long influence in the history of science, but again it inspired and guided by resonance but without intelligible form. "Oriented Relations" (OR) establishes its structure through reason and sets it firaly in the present physical realm. That essential form discloses the universal source and spiritual ground of the mystic experience, which Einstein referred to as "the source of all true art and science".

The germinal concept being introduced is that the "mystic experience" is real, it is a personal involvement in a physical property of the universe. This realization led to expressing the structure of the universe through a universal essence that extends from its formal framework being developed by physics and science in general, while supporting a unitive continuity within the universe that includes all matter, applies most intensely in living entities, and continues focusing in humans as a potential spiritual experience supported by consciousness. The scope of this integration generates a clarity and stability in each, relatively radical insights, and a synthesis of concerns that have long been independent and often conflicting dimensions in the history of our cultures. Reason is respected and maintained throughout and its structure presents the "mystic" experience as logical and integral, therein offering an accessible portal towards a further expansion of our self-identity.

The universal essence is a State, a set of conditions integrating as a system, this is the State of Relation (S of R). The essential State requires relating entities, it does not exist without physical interaction. The general form of the S of R is presented through three basic properties. The first is that its descriptive dimension respects its nature and fertility best when given as spacetime (ST). In OR, ST applies to a dynamic phenomenon; ST is an insightful analytical convention but it is not discrete, the phenomenon is discrete and manifests its essential State. The S of R is depicted most simply by the root-metaphor of the two-bodied relation of Celestial Mechanics. The second property is that the essential State is fundamentally a form: the defining phenomenon develops from physical properties of the *Orientor* and those properties extend in its State to an *Oriented;* the S of R is oriented. This also suggests that the essential State expands to the physical universe as similar but more complex involvements of the root-metaphor. The third property is that the essential State creates a unity of its participants. OR is a unique form of action-at-a-distance; a concrete example of the S of R is the Earth-Moon system in its solar orbit.

ST is the optimal descriptive dimension because the essential State is inherently dynamic. This exists beyond the abstract most concretely and inclusively as a defining condition of the systems within and unified as the universe. The nature of our solar system, a simplified version of the universe, is also an effective agent in evolution, and essential form, innate dynamism, and relational participation are major characteristics in the nature of all lifeforms. The evolutionary process is the extension of an entity's relational form through an eventual intensification of some aspect of those involvements, which expands that specific influence within its system to slowly reorganize as a more complex and intense entity. The most intense human S of R is consciousness; its awareness of our essential inclusion and congruency within the universal Unity is a spiritual property, its property evolved from cosmic harmony and order as a resonant awareness is reason. And the harmony of reason can begin us towards universal belonging. Order can tend towards organization, which can tend towards efficiency, which can extend onward, this is a fundamental characteristic of our evolutionary process. In consciousness efficiency is the efforts of understanding towards simple yet fertile clarity. Once conceptually recognized in the world around us, the universal essence can expand its presence inward and outward. And the essential State applying concretely, variously, universally and simultaneously, presents *Reality*. This suggests the direction in which OR will develop.

 A primary concern of OR is to clarify and intensify our personal participation in the universal essential State. To move towards that realization we will take a quick glance at the essential State in its involvements as matter, light, and then consciousness; this can ground and broaden the nature of ST form. Matter's S of R manifests as material bodies relating in a dynamic Unity, and it is absolute, every body of matter is in an immediate relational State with every other body, however distant, minute, or dense it is, although in ST form the effect of an Orientor is diminished by distance of separation. This most basic State exists without a setup process or material trajectory required to create or sustain it. The unity of each State and the unitive whole of the universe as interrelating States, are both absolute; their ST phenomenon of inherent dynamism is formal motion. The magnitude of that inherent motion is generated by properties of each State's Orientor. This inherent motion is inertial, meaning that the existence of the motion is force-free, an aspect of the dynamic form of its essential State. The two basic types of formal motion are orbital and radial, which present the two inertial components of ST form. Radial motion has been presented as caused by a force of gravity; in OR when it exists it is formally inertial, it does not involve a causal force. Elliptical orbits and all "non-orbital motions" include the influence of the two inertial components, the transverse and radial. The transverse exists perpendicular to the axis of the State and conceptually considered relative to the circular orbit at that distance, and the radial moves relative to the Orientor along the axis of its State.

An Orientor's properties establish the velocity for circular inertia at each radial distance, and this transverse motion functions as a reference by establishing the ideal "energy" of that specific body's orbit. Without a transverse motion the Oriented moves as an inertial "falling body", moving at the acceleration rate of the Orientor applying within the form of its S of R; if the transverse motion is the Orientor's circular value at that radial distance it orbits in an inertial circle, and no radial component exists. If a body's orbit has a transverse motion greater than the circular value at its closest perpendicular distance, it is at periapsis with a radial inertial component directed away from the Orientor, reducing the elevated energy of the State due to the increased radial distance. And this is a formal influence not a force. As the orbital energy continues to decrease the Oriented will either move in an elliptical orbit or pass by. All natural motion is either orbital, radial or merely passing by. An elliptical orbit will eventually again become perpendicular to the radial axis, it's then at apoapsis in a low energy position with a radial component that is now directed towards the Orientor increasing its orbital motion, it will then reach another orbital periapsis. In OR a simple falling body's S of R begins from arrested motion and accelerates towards its Orientor at the formal ST radial rate. The circular orbit defines the ideal inherent dynamism at that radial distance; in non-circular orbits the magnitude of the orbital motion manifests the radial inertia, which basically has a corrective energy function in its State. The magnitudes of the two inertial motions is formal, they are not influenced by the mass of the orbiting body. In a circular orbit there is no centripetal or centrifugal force, in elliptical orbits they are conventions labeling the result of radial inertia. The inherent dynamism is the substance of ST form, the universal essence defines its structure, and the Orientor determines its formal values. All essential States can exist or not exist, all except the relational State of Matter, which necessarily exists and is therefore the physical source of the inherent dynamism of the Universe. A circular inertial orbit is the ideal image of Matter's S of R. This is a simplified sketch of Matter's ST form; the basic mathematics of the sketch is presented at the end of this work. In OR an action-at-a-distance has an axis *within its essential State*, denoting the extended continuity of that unitive system, this might have appeased Einstein's attitude rejecting spooky action-at-a-distance. OR is a focus on aspects of Einstein's conception.

> On Tides. Simplified model: the Earth is in a counterclockwise circular orbit around the Sun, and has a counterclockwise rotation. The orbital motion is determined at the Earth's center of mass, but the Earth's surface water has a motion that differs from the orbital yet it is in the same essential State. Along a line through the two centers of mass, the furthest surface water has a relative motion greater than the orbital and the closest water motion is in the opposite direction and is less. The furthest motion, like the condition at periapsis, will have an inertial vector directed away from the Sun, and the closest motion will have a vector directed towards the Sun. This produces the two tides.
> Assume the Moon has a counterclockwise circular orbit around the Earth and no rotation. The water is now on the Orientor adding to its ST properties as additional "energy" yet its fluidity responds in the existing essential S of R. Along the extended axis of the State, both the nearest and farthest rotating water are moving with higher energy than the orbital condition and both have a vector away from the Orientor. This causes the two tides. The traditional explanation of the tidal effects of both Moon and Sun, uses their gravitational force for the nearest tide and an apparent "centrifugal force" for the furthest. A centrifugal force is called a "fictitious" possibility in Newtonian mechanics, it solves problems and explains but limits the consistency and natural scope of the conception.

The "weightlessness" of astronaut and spacecraft is often explained as being caused by their continuous gravitational "free fall" within the orbit. At the optimal velocity an Oriented would be falling at the same rate as the Earth's curvature, therefore the circular orbit. This is presented using the Newtonian model of straight-line inertia and a gravitational force. Einstein's ST continuum rejects a "force" of gravity, the force-free motion is following the curvature of a ST continuum. In OR the weightlessness is due to the force-free inertial orbit determined by properties of the Orientor in essential ST form. This depicts the common practice of using whatever conventions and theoretical models are available to solve problems and simplify understanding; this is clearly legitimate, but it continues to disregard the universal form as their context, which offers a scope of an underlying unitive condition. OR presents the universe as an inherently dynamic holistic unity, with a defining essential State that extends to apply to all physical entities, and conceptually and personally to each of us. The essential State manifests the physical and formal conditions that our focused conventions describe and explain.

> Do not misunderstand the intension here, our use of conventions and analytical systems were and are obviously necessary for the enormous successes of science and technology. But Reality also exists free of intellectual impositions, and the simplicity of OR is being presented as the ground of science and human spirituality, which are today clarified, objectified, and potentially unified by reason. Consider a river adapted to grind grain, or the wind and sunlight to generate electricity, all were achieved through the insights of science. But they still remain the river, the wind and the sunlight, each a very fertile experience in Nature. OR develops from the formal universe underlying our conventions.

Consider a light Source. Its ST properties extend within the unifying form of its essential State to all Objects accessible to an axis. The inherent dynamism of light as radiation is presented by its frequencies (f) with intensities (I) and wavelengths (λ), which are inner properties of the Orientor-Source, not discrete entities. A light State has a ST extension defined by the combined energies of (f), (I) and (λ), which are diminished by distance, but unlike Matter's State, the light State requires a setup process, light's unity can be extinguished, orbital inertia cannot. We have referred to that process as the "velocity of light" (c), but in OR (c) is the universal setup velocity for essential States, and completes as a continuous pulse at the Object along the axis of the State, establishing normal essential conditions. The universal speed is maintained by the adjustment of defining components within the form of its State, as (λ and f). The frequency shifts towards the red with distance due to ST form, but "c" maintains its formal constancy. In OR there is no material trajectory from Source to Object. Due to its universal speed the setup duration is distance dependent, but once the extension is established the State maintains its unitive pressure as immediacy until terminated. Immediacy reflects in setup States the absolute characteristic of ST form observed in Matter's more fundamental and absolute State.

> It is said that the axis of a light S of R will be bent when passing near the Sun. This implies that a State's axis has some degree of "effective substance", and this would not only apply to the light's axis but to the range of axes from the widely relating Sun that the light passes through causing a slight refraction; as Einstein implied, energy

is a form of mass. This possibility is said to also be suggested by spectrographic analysis.

The *camera obscura* is an analog of an isolated eye, both are on Objects that are in a distant dependent S of R with secondary Sources; the hole and pupil are openings in their "Object" that extend the State inward. The eye further continues its setup process by extending that State as input to the mind, which like the eye is a component of consciousness. Traditional theory presents light as invisible massless "particles of waves", as photons or quanta from a Source bombarding Objects that then become secondary Sources that radiate their own frequencies as color, tone, brightness, etc., again as particle-waves, to other Objects or to an Observer's eye. In the eye they impinge the retina to form an image that is extended on. This model would reduce consciousness to the interpretation of images upon the retina, as if watching a movie. This isolates consciousness from any direct visual and personal involvement with the actual world. In OR an illuminated Object establishes a unitive S of R at the eye, and the process is continued on as consciousness. Consciousness becomes the Orientor of a reverse S of R, with inner properties such as knowledge, intelligence and sensibility that define our awareness through the eye and mind, intensifying the unitive State with its original Source and the outside world. Consciousness is an experience of the real world through its developed properties; the eye establishes the range and focus of sight. The S of R is the means of sight, not emitted particles. This conception combines both of our history's conflicting models of sight, as intromission and as extromission.

Considering Einstein' Photoelectric Effect. A light S of R exists from a Source to every Object accessible to an axis, in this case to the entire surface of a sheet of metal. The influence of light in the visible range translates directly to the Object's surface color and temperature. When higher frequencies are used (in the ultraviolet or above), free electrons of the metal are emitted. In OR the extending pulse or flux input causes the ejection, this has also been interpreted as momentum. Every metal has a threshold value as the minimum amount of energy required to eject electrons. Another factor determining the amount of ejection is the location of an electron within the metal, which is especially influenced by its depth from the surface. In OR the irradiation is a property of the S of R, not a particle-wave trajectory's momentum. Increasing the Intensity of the frequency would influence the depth of energy penetration, causing more electrons to be emitted.

The S of R as the universal essence focuses consciousness towards expanding the scope of both Reality and our own essential S of R. Consciousness has a potential for an outward-inward resonance in the natural world through the Unity it is a part of, with a further potential towards developing an expanded self-identity that can strengthen our awareness and support the rational structure and personal involvement of our investigations and theories. In OR Reality is exhibited by the recognized and realized examples of the essential S of R existing locally and throughout the universe, most vividly and variably as lifeforms. Ultimate Reality is the omnipresent essential State itself, within the universal Unity it generates; our spirituality is the personal experience of Reality, Ultimate Reality, or the Unity. This presents a natural and rational tendency towards the ancient experience of self-inclusive Oneness. The recognition of our essential S of R having analogs throughout Nature is an optimal spiritual opportunity. And our historical precedent for Ultimate Reality, Reality, its Unity, and our personal spiritual participation, is religion.

There are many today, and especially in science, that equate spirituality with the supernatural and the dangerous fanatical bias extending beyond preference as "ours vs theirs". OR offers an inclusive spiritual form with an accessible means towards that involvement without dogma or theology, this could expand human awareness and intensify the consciousness of Our Time.

A universal essence that respects, intensifies, and integrates both our investigation of the physical realm and our personal participation in its ultimate nature, can successfully simplify and clarify a Way, because truth is "of Our Time" within a personal involvement in Reality. When only one perspective of the integration is respected and focused upon, there is eventually a temporary suspension of conceptual progress and a tendency towards extravagant imaginations. A very successful way is to apply our analytical conventions towards problem solving and increased understanding, while realizing that they are conventions. This can distinguish our analyses and applications from simple and immediate Reality as a potential spiritual experience while maintaining respect for both. Gathered information will always aid in developing truth, but it requires the context of harmonious consistency and unitive form to achieve Truth. Our physics, as it evolved has today entered a system that temporarily faces a wall of "counterintuitive" conceptions and analytical models, with significant technological applications and results; we often attempt further extensions of this "accepted irrationality" through logical possibility. In OR the common denominator of the two criteria of Truth is the universal essence, the S of R. Historically mankind has investigated the actual world to the best of our abilities while respecting Reality through various belief systems that honored Ultimate Reality but could not approach It through reason, therefore we used poetry and imaginative narrative to Truthfully acknowledge, respect, and bond in the awareness of that real Presence. Reason is not a religion but it can be spiritual. Today we must distinguish between legitimate means toward spirituality, and spirituality as a degree of personal resonance. The "mystic experience" was considered to be "beyond understanding", and often as supernatural, this limited our participation and creative efforts towards clarifying Truth and intensifying our self-identity. We must move on.

> "The religion of the future will be a cosmic religion. It should transcend a personal God and avoid dogma and theology. Covering both the natural and the spiritual, it should be based on a religious sense arising from the experience of all things, natural and spiritual, as a meaningful unity" .
>
> —Albert Einstein

Implications of OR

"When he speaks of 'truth' the layman usually means something obvious and well-know, whereas it seems to me that one of the most important and extremely difficult task of our time is to work on elaborating a new idea of Truth. That is also what I mean when I always emphasize that science and religion, like *truth* and *Truth*, must be related in some way through our spirituality".

—Wolfgang Pauli

Formal inherent dynamism has broad implications. OR sketches Reality without relying on conventions such as causal forces, particles, waves or an ether, and in OR inertia is not an independent force resisting acceleration, not a discrete ST continuum distorted by mass, not a Natural Law, it is a formal property of Matter's essential S of R. But the major characteristic of Reality and Being that OR introduces is their common essential nature offering personal Unity.

Parmenides was a 6th Century BCE pre-Socratic philosopher.

"Parmenides' question, Is Reality One or Many?
Parmenides' answer, One.
Parmenides' explanation, *the many* is a delusion of our senses, the One is experienced by a deeper ability."

—John Mansley Robinson
in *An Introduction to Early Greek Philosophy*

Dr. Robinson expanded on this, "The closing of this gap, the union of thought and being, involves a knowing which differs not merely in degree but in kind from ordinary knowing…" "But in Parmenides this religious vision is joined with a passion for logic that distinguishes him at once from his successors …"

OR is the fusion of these two kinds of knowing. One is intellectual the other is a spiritual experience grounded in but ultimately independent of information. To respect this State of naturalism OR applies reason to intellectually present the unity of Reality that includes each of us and all around us, easing mind towards recognized congruity. But then we must transcend the learning to free spiritually towards resonance as the Unity we belong within and are as Being.

"Time" in OR. This presentation concerning "time" begins by acknowledging that there will be two perspectives necessarily involved. We start with the inherent dynamism of the unified universe. The second perspective is the realization that life has evolved influenced by our immediate solar system within the universe, and all lifeforms have characteristic of that dynamic system assimilated and modified within their nature. Through evolution life has temporal characteristics derived from the universal Source, such as the inertial orbital periods, and human consciousness can realize and apply this innate sensibility as "time". This is possible because we also have developed a unique capacity for self-awareness, which is a very fertile attribute, but at today's stage of development it has a dangerous tendency towards self-absorbed egocentricity, yet it could also turn our attention towards Nature and broadened our sense of self-identity.

Cosmic inherent dynamism differs drastically from the assimilated temporal dimensions in evolved entities. Inertial motion, as the inherent dynamism of Matter's universal essence, always maintains its formal constancy as Matter's S of R, whereas an evolved entity will develop new variations of relatability and inherent dynamism that fundamentally alter its essential State. Consciousness can apply its intrinsic temporal awareness as *standardized units* and as *past-present-future* on the world because they have been manifested within our nature, but they do not realistically exist in the universe prior to evolution, that is, in the cosmic system independent of consciousness and life in general. "Time" is used to describe, measure, and analyze inherent dynamism and natural order in the universe through change, the universe changes but always s maintains as Matter's dynamic S of R, altering locally in magnitude and complexity but always essentially absolute as the unities and Unity it is. And the Unity of the universe never requires a new setup process. All lifeforms have a temporal dimension in their nature that physically varies its State through continuing to grow and intensify from birth to death, whereas the universe itself does not formally change *in time*, it formally functions *as time,* as absorbed, observed and applied by consciousness. The celestial universe is uncaused.

Consider a planet with a circularly orbiting moon, this is to us both a clock and an inherently dynamic unitive entity. The present universe is a variation of that entity, its essential form remains constant within its unity. And realized form is one of our most fertile means towards knowledge and Truth; innate form is the quiet quality of Reality. Inherent dynamism is the condition manifesting the formal interactions of relating matter. "Time" is applied by consciousness by imposing its own inner characteristics and devised conventions as useful tools towards a better understanding of natural harmony and order. Today we begin an alternative that frees consciousness from the tyranny of those applied tools while continuing to use them, but now with expanded awareness. To apply time to States prior to evolution is interesting as a discussion, but to impose time as an absolute conceptual dimension there, is a distortion of that essential unity and a display of egocentricity, which can impose a mist on our further intensification of awareness. No Big Bang Beginning, no First Cause, and no expanding universe. Change in that State exists as a response to other bodies, as observed by consciousness. This disregard of absolute linear time is not an imposition of ignorance, it is a realization with a holistic scope, an opportunity leading to insights that free and extend the personal resonance of intellectual and spiritual involvement. In Eastern religions, freeing the mind of ego distortions, current events, and information during meditation more readily leads inner calm towards Being.

A clarification on "rejecting the accelerated expansion of the universe". We will consider three main explanations often given for the "expansion's" redshift. The cosmological redshift says that the distance of separation of Source and Observer could present the Big Bang expansion even if their separation is physically constant: the duration of light between them increases in a unitive expansion, as would the frequency. In OR the redshift would apply to the frequency of a stationary Source as observed by a stationary Observer, and in ST form the greater the distance of separation the greater the redshift.

A motion of Source or Object does affect the duration of a S of R, but some physicists say that expansion could bring about a redshift due to a Doppler Effect. The Doppler Effect in sound is a common experience. In OR the redshift is formal and normal within a S of R, without expansion.

A light S of R is setup when an axis exists. There are two ways to picture the setup process. One is that the 3-dimensional pulse exists at the Source and extends as ST form to unify with the Object-at-a-distance, the other is that the duration of the process is distance dependent but comes into existence all at once at completion, because it is the normal condition of an essential State. And however established, the illumination has some degree of effective "substance" as a relatively weak radial effect at the Object referred to as the "light pressure", caused by the components of the pulse. Light pressure is small but must be acknowledged when plotting extraterrestrial projectile paths. Once setup, light's S of R remains immediate until obstructed.

The essential S of R is the core dimension of evolution, culminating in us as consciousness integrating all of the relational capacities of body and mind. Once our State is setup, we relate visually to actual Objects in the real world, and now immediately without delay. This includes Sources at "light year" distances, we see them in a common moment, in a common "now". I have read that "if we were thousands of light years away and could see the Earth, we might see dinosaurs wandering about"; not so. Immediacy is a normal property throughout the Unity of the material universe, and once setup that same effect would exist in the States of light and sight. (And this characteristic seems relevant to quantum entanglement).

The State of Relation has roots in the model of Einstein's ST Continuum, The setup speed remains a constant in all States of Relation, for all distances of separation, and it is not affected by a motion of Source or Object, which only alters the length of the axis and therefore the duration of the setup process. For example, a motion of a complete light S of R system in the direction of the Object would extend the distance of the axis during setup and therefore extend the setup duration, the opposite motion of that State would "contract" the duration. This alteration of duration is real but it applies to the specific measuring device (as a light-clock) not to some dimension of Absolute Time. Such a "time dilation" would not apply to life's processes.

> Einstein setup this analysis in a freely falling box. A pulse of light from the top of the box to the bottom would be longer than a pulse from the bottom to the top. Clocks positioned at the top and bottom, both using its light duration as the unit of time, would differ. But again, it is the measuring devices that vary not some absolute dimension of time.

In OR the redshift causes of "cosmological motion", a "Doppler effect", or an unnecessary "presence of unobservable Dark Matter", are misleading. Adding motion (as ST) to a body would add mass (as ST); adding ST as motion to an atomic clock would slow the rate of decay and therefore its measurements. In OR once various States of sight are setup to an Object they are completed, and all could then see immediately all available aspects of that Source. Therefore simultaneity *does* exist. Mercury has an elliptical orbit, the velocity at perihelion will be greater than the circular inertial value at that distance; the orbital velocity will have a radial component directed away from the Sun. This will delay the point of perihelion, causing precession.

Our State of consciousness can begin towards resonance within the Unity of Reality through the consistent harmony of our ideas and conceptions as reason. Harmony and order present objective poetry, they reach far beyond their local application, and we can become consistent with the immediate real, as profoundly presented in high Tang Dynasty poetry. A primary impact of OR is in its scope, which today extends from an uncaused universe to its inner resonant unity that exists through the universal essence we belong within and ultimately are. When experimental results violate reason we should consider this as a rich opportunity to reinvestigate the theories structuring our interpretations, accepting irrationality as actual violates the nature of Reality, our evolutionary heritage, and our essential nature. And irrational theory is a hindrance to the intensification of consciousness. OR is a celebration of the fundamental harmony of Reality, with a historical precedent as "the Harmony of the Spheres". Pythagoras was a prophet of Form, and his leap of insight was triggered by the relationships of numerical ratio in music composition and its performance on strings: as the fusion of the act of performance of Art and its creative presentation. This he further extended to the spatial relationship of planets and the cosmos. The broadest description of the essence of Reality is "the structure of universal form", and essential form can function as a preexisting chord in intellectual investigations. Without that ground we aggressively grope about in illogical possibilities, with it we can face the unknown with a sense of fertile familiarity. This could be labeled "metaphysics", but it must not remain "meta-", it is most important as a symbiotic quality within creative thought and artistic efforts, more significant in its personal rhyme than as philosophical abstraction or as a source of questions or discussion. The symbiosis further strengthens and grows as knowledge and awareness expand. This can draw us towards a new component of consciousness, long known but historically experienced only in uniquely singular moments or through intense spiritual commitment. Today the "mystic experience" should be seen as a rational potential that can develop towards expanding our self-identity as a conscious resonance within Reality, personally, and through effort supportive of the Way of others.

The potential for experiencing the universal Unity intensifies through recognizing our essential State related to that of entities throughout Nature, and this can extend on to a broader bonding with and in, the absolute Unity of the universe. These relational States throughout Nature congruous with our own are not poetic conceits they are objective facts that challenge our personal awareness much like conceits. And ancient Oneness is no longer merely a poetic term, it's a fact that might best be presented poetically to reflect its harmonious and fertile nature. Ultimate Reality exists as a formal Presence independent of specificity and analysis, but creative efforts focus its coherence and accessibility, widening the potential for its experience through recognizing the form of its all-inclusive essence, becoming an image of our own nature. Truth often begins as information but fulfills personally, and we achieve that transcendence best through "doing", through focused efforts. Rational spirituality opens our modern destiny; religion is our heritage and continues as a positive means towards spiritual awareness and personal morality. OR stresses the scope of our spiritual nature, its humanistic concerns are left to cultural adaptations of the Golden Rule applied through commonsense and common decency.

"In The Beginning" is the inherently dynamic uncaused timeless universe. OR develops from that unitive State

through the key word "Reality", a term often dismissed as too vague to have objective significance, but it is no longer vague, Reality is generated by the universal essence, the S of R, which includes us and everything observed. The cosmic Unity the essence creates is the Source of the nature of consciousness, reason, and the quality of our spirituality. A major culmination of OR is to suggest the ground, structure, and vision of Nature as a rational spiritual Presence. This existential context has quietly begun to form and lurk in the ambience of Our Time. Science could extend this structure through the continuity of reason far beyond the accepted limitations of material and specialized concerns, to further harmonize our personal sphere with the cosmic sphere. The form of that relationship has traditionally been honored and guided by religion; and unitive form will always be a source, means, and achievement of high Art. We need a vista of personal congruency infusing the consciousness of Our Time with a sense of universal belonging, offering the ease to seek, find, and be our spiritual nature through whatever means we find fertile. Spiritual being is a personal achievement, religion and reason are fertile means. And a specific vectored or rambled Way as our personal route, is our life.

> "I am a deeply religious nonbeliever.
> This is a somewhat new kind of religion".
>
> —Albert Einstein

An Epilogue

Any means offering spiritual resonance as a peak personal experience through its approximation of the nature of Reality, Ultimate Reality, or Universal Unity justifies its Way. But my concern here is not the Ultimate State but the quality of the methods within their means. Reason has a natural rhyme towards the Unity, but its method through mental focus is not a fertile means for everyone. And rational structure has a certain kind of beauty but in terms of spiritual satisfaction it can appear bland from a distance. Compare it to Negro spirituals in a neighborhood Church, the ancient tribal dances and harmony in Nature of Native American cultures, the daily formal commitment of Muslims, a Jew's moment of quiet alone with their history, ancient and modern, and the unique social, cultural and mental support for a wide range of religions throughout India. But reason's form offers a more obvious possibility to many, which can intensify to probability and become personalized through creative thought and action. Emotional involvement and physical rituals can certainly enhance spirituality, and every religion has a spiritual awareness within the dogma and theology of its belief system, but history and surely modern history, has shown that a highly emotional spirituality can become a dangerously biased passion when only righteous dogma defines a believer's spirituality rather than personal resonance.

Reason as a resonant involvement of intellect has an obvious consistency within its natural method. It lacks the emotional beauty and drama of religions but it builds a more readily accessible, objective, and organically involved means. Today a recognition of universal form throughout Nature can lead mind to a congruency with other relational States in its immediate locale, which can eventually tend towards the experience of the Unity of Reality. This is an alternative Way, but its rational structure supports every major religion. We can live at ease within its scope: from an uncaused origin to the eternal essence that defines and unifies us with every entity we immediately and creatively realize. And very little imagination is required to see the parallel between OR and Theism. We all should know that Reality is objectively spiritual.

The Basic Mathematics of the Inertial Components of ST Form

$v_r^2 = r_r g_r$ circular orbital motion, which as mv_r^2 becomes our convention of "energy" at "r"

$g_r = g_s (R_s/r_r)^2$ radial inertial component of ST form, more generally, an Orientor's inverse-square function

$v_r^2 = g_s (R_s^2/r_r)$ transverse inertial component of ST form, which as mv_r^2 is an alternate expression of its "energy".

Subscript "r" applies to circular orbits, and subscript "s" applies to the Orientor; (r) is the distance from the center of the Orientor to the center of the Oriented; (g) is the radial acceleration of ST form (not the result of a gravitational force).

"All of these endeavors are based on the belief that existence should have a completely harmonious structure. Today, we have less ground than ever before for allowing ourselves to be forced away from this wonderful belief."

—Albert Einstein

Notes

Inertial orbits underlie the inherent dynamism and uncaused condition of the universe. The force-free, self-perpetuating, self-regulating and unifying system that is the universe can also be seen as the ground Source of all lifeforms; its formal dynamism can generate evolutionary processes in isolated States, imposing an inner temporal dimensions in each. The universe can appear much like the image of an ancient god, as the ultimate Source of all that is living, and through its essential unity all that is spiritual. And She slowly continues and intensifies her fertile processes and insights, Age after Age.

On the spirituality of physics. In the text I quote only Einstein and Pauli, but I could have also quoted Niels Bohr, Schrodinger, and Heisenberg, many were deeply aware of a spiritual presence in physics.

OR and the Axial Age

In 1949 the German philosopher Karl Jaspers introduced the term "Axial Age", as applying to a pivotal period in human history from approximately 900 BCE to 200 BCE, with its peak around 550 BCE. During this period mankind developed a broader more focused approach to human self-identity, and this basic change occurred independently in India, China, Persia, and Greece without significant dialogue between the cultures. In the 6th Century BCE religious development formalized and sustained: Hinduism, Buddhism, and Jainism in India, Confucianism and Taoism in China, Zoroastrianism in Persia as a prime influence on Judaism, Christianity, and Islam, and simultaneously with these occurred the great natural philosophers of Greece. Major minds developed in each culture that had a lasting effect on their science, philosophy and religions through drastically changing the aware participation of a human life regarding how we perceived of ourselves and the world around us. The broadest characteristic of that change was the intensification of self-awareness and personal responsibility through the reorientation of major concerns from establishing common cultural norms to focusing personal realizations. The period began reducing the presence of myth as an effective agent and turning to a more analytical approach, resulting in a reconsideration of accepted certainties and attitudes through a more direct involvement in the physical world. This also brought about a deepening of regard for the quality and accountability of a life within the context of free-will, for example each of the core cultures developed its own version of the Golden Rule. Nature became more secular and objectified, science and philosophy were stimulated and began to be formalized through a deepened respect for reason, which extended on towards logic and methodology. Much excellent scholarly work has been done concerning this germinal period because of its deep and lasting influence on human history. One defect of the Axial Age often noted was that it was strongly patriarchal, during this period social unrest and conflict were widespread, and the Warrior remained primary in the establishment of social priorities, with a resulting devaluation of women as a voice determining human values.

There is today an interpretation of our Time as the beginning of a New Axial Age due to the achievements in the sciences and the broadening of human awareness, such as through biology, brain studies, genetics, medicine, psychology, and cosmology; other dimensions often mentioned are the cultural interactions cultivating globalization, an increased responsibility concerning the conservation and stewardship of Nature, and a deepened respect for the feminine perspective. And the more vocal voices for a New Axial Age are often religious scholars stressing broadened spiritual concerns. OR presents Our Time as a prelude to another expansive leap in our evolution, very similar to the result of the Axial Age, where today Ultimate Reality can become objective, a personal experience rather than a personified Image or mystical enigma. This could imply a general direction of human evolution through a common means of development from a common source, physically and historically, and even suggest a common personal goal, especially as it applies in our own life. These implications are logical results in OR.

OR begins a bridgework towards a further stage in human evolution as another intensification and extension of our self-identity. The means of realizing this new degree of personal expansion is the universal essence as the State of Relation. The most fundamental form of the universal essence is Matter's State, which is absolute and uncaused, thereby establishing the absolute ground of the Unity of Reality and our conceptualizations towards it, focused through our inclusion in it. Our manifestation of the universal essence is consciousness. The new stage of self-expansion is actually quite ancient as a respected awareness, it was most clearly acknowledged and stressed in the spirituality of Eastern religions. What makes Our Time unique is that we can now present the nature of this evolutionary extension through reason by enunciating its physical source, structure, and scope as our personal congruency. This will have a cogent and supportive effect in science and philosophy. The universal Presence of the unitive essence is Ultimate Reality, and it is now accessible to experience beyond belief and ritual through reason. Not only is consciousness an example of that universal essence, our capacity for extending understanding is analogous with and enriched by the Unity the essence generates. Our congruency has within it a transcendent potential for the physical Unity, as a possibility to momentarily merge our being within the Unity. This participation of consciousness is ultimately a touch of fusion with the universe as Being, which is today a very rare experience, but the knowledge of human congruency is not beyond today's common sensibility and intelligence. An immediate opportunity to know and develop this awareness is through Nature, where every living entity is a S of R as an evolutionary variation of our own essence. This offers a sense of expanding self-awareness through realizing and indwelling exterior stages of consistency. An excellent metaphor expressing the ultimate fusion is in the ancient Upanishads of the early Axial Age, as "a drop of water falling into the sea"; it has also been recognized in many religions as an experience of Oneness. And the universal essence we example and ultimately are, continues in the real world after our death, which offers another resonant realization within the uncaused universe. If we consider the Axial Age as a refocusing of self-awareness and personal responsibility, we can continue our evolution as an extension towards a moment of unitive participation by nurturing our realizations and actions.

Words merely represent, they are our convention of communication, yet they can structure a social portal composed of awareness and realizations directing, clarifying, and vivifying their author and receptive others towards the spiritual experience. Human spirituality is the awareness of our essential inclusion in Reality, and it intensifies towards an experience of identity. We can change "me as self" to extend as "that which I am", and begin finding our own Way. Supernaturalism and reincarnation are valid means supporting a religious person's Way; they should be treated as myth only when they are seen as personal hindrances. And "God" will long remain an excellent Image of Ultimate Reality, but our earliest deities were often female, goddesses of fertility extending on as the source and core of family and home. We must cherish that quality and expand its richness into the momentum of our evolution. The purpose of life is to find spiritual contentment and deepened happiness through any means personally acceptable, to then live secure in our Reality. This is the solid ground of human fulfillment.

On My Poetry

"Science arose from poetry—when times change the two can meet again on a higher level as friends".

—Johann Wolfgang von Goethe

My poetry has roots in the Metaphysical poetry of the 17 Century. It's basically a personal voice, using language that is close to conversational rather than rising from heartfelt sensitivity; its content is structured in reason and logic rather than the imagery and dramatic effect of our most memorable poetry; its most successful inspiration is intellectual rather than emotional. But the unique characteristic of my poetry is that it is predicated on my prose work "OR, An Alternative". Although the Way it suggests could be described as guided by resonant conceits, the form of the conceits are as facts waiting to be realized. The future it presents is spiritually Artistic, while supported by Science.

> A poem can also tone the mind
> by honing sensibility;
> we can then roam the raw unknown
> with a scent of recognition,
> the hard and cold can melt and flow
> a warming glow of consonance.
>
> Communion in poetry
> is guided by our inner sense,
> we ignore, misinterpret

or mentally feed on this
depending on our resonance.
Even unheard by cluttered mind
a poem can rest in quiet peace,
like an old overgrown Temple
hushed by twisted vine and debris
awaiting archeology.

> *...planets move in quiet dark;*
> *a midnight rose, a silent lark*

A poem can ring deeper than fact
it's built through rhyme and symmetry;
facts must meld backward
before they grope onward,
a poem blends on quite naturally.

Evolution is concrete poetry,
core form shaped from inner States
slowly induces minor traits
that intensify and integrate.
Like a bloom compressed as a bud
or a root from an old crusted seed,
mind can expand to rise and be
a source of reflective beauty.

> *... in quiet dark the planets move*
> *the midnight rose, the silent lark...*

A poem's insight can vivify
what music more easily mimes
and celebrates. Art rising high
can support a well-tempered mind;
working a cosmic vision

vectors its participation.
Earned insight will chime deep
beyond a learned repeat,
echoing as congruency;
reason and its logic
as pure artistic acts
can state local conceits
as self-expanding facts
to a fertile mind
eager to find
by roaming the Tao of its Time.

Poetry reflects and respects
our informing experience;
a poem can naturally share
the spiritual when expressed
in lines addressing open minds
by baring the real truthfully,
each awareness can then extend
as its own Way swells and blends.

Offering Art personally
can quicken human consciousness
through the common kinships shown,
but of equal significance
to those creating attuned, alone,
we grow, nurture, and tone our own.

> *The midnight rose, that silent lark*
> *like floating moons of planets viewed,*
> *send forth their song*
> *in the light of dawn*
> *and grace our life as Nature's muse.*

My Introduction

Crawled, out of swamp, and I rested.
Here and now I'm alive alone
with solid ground beneath me.
I sit with near peaks grand and clear
others misted in distance.
I sit, relaxed, in my own here.

Resting settles to awareness;
I've arrived to start. I'll seek flow
within the sense of winding stream
finding the natural way,
being a means of spreading green
to eager minds with roots reaching,
feeding their fertility
towards being a natural need.

I know a brook flow can broaden
fulfilling as pools of belief
or as spirit's deep calming sea:
    cosmically curved yet seen level
    by cultures viewing through their faith
    a universal quality.
We will pass through homely village
and noisy city dulled to all
but busy jobs and leisure's pleasures.

Living free needs active effort
enhancing cherished solitude,

    to then rest in transcendent fugue
    with the quietude of Nature.
    The water from peaks arrives clear,
    each peak an icon of the Presence
       its white the source of stream
       the stream a source of a Way
       my Way a source of me
       me my sense of Reality.
    I stood my strength erect and walked,
    through birdsong shade of living trees
    spreading their calm nobility;
    I'm on my Way.

    But I know my current began
    long ago, in early childhood.

My father died when I was four, he committed suicide. My Mother never remarried, she preferred to work and she was skilled and diligent. She advanced from local, to regional, to large city, and on to the University of Minnesota as a secretary-financial research assistant. I lived with her parents in an Iron Mining village during my youth. They spoke no English, I spoke no Serbian; we communicated well enough. I entertained myself. When my Mother returned on vacations she often read to me, most memorably from "The Wisdom of China and India" by Lin Yutang. My early favorite was the Ramayana, about Rama, Sita and that "monkey guy". She later referred to "Cosmic Consciousness", and Teilhard de Chardin, both were in our library; I eventually skimmed through them. And her classical music established a solid home in my life. My Mother was my family and a permanent influence. During my youth I returned to the East's various sources of vision and wisdom, seldom with learning but always with deep respect. Something was there.

> I did not often comprehend
> but I maintained an inner sense
> that was readily dulled by youth,
> a youth free to unchecked wildness
> eases into loud shallowness;
> the Eastern truths laid as a lump
> not of learned vision or wisdom
> but like a seed dropped in my dark,
> a weight lurking a lack in me.

I was active in high school sports. During my junior year I was arrested and jailed twice for drunk and disorderly. The Iron Range has been referred to as one of the last regions in the U.S. to establish Law and Order; I could get a drink in a dancehall since 10th grade. My senior year was spent at a military academy, a type of Reform School. After a year of college engineering I joined the Navy. The Korean War was my stated purpose but for two years I was a whitehat in a Fighter Squadron on the East Coast, with Carrier cruises to the Mediterranean, North Atlantic, and Caribbean. I was given a Captain's Mast for drunk and disorderly, breaking arrest, and threatening a Shore Patrol, I spent 5 days in a Marine Brig. I was then shipped off to Aviation Electronics School in Memphis where, before graduation, I was given a Summary Court Marshall by the stunted runt of a Station Captain for "smoking in the barracks" and because, I was told, my record was noted "not recommended for reenlistment": the "Uniform Code of Military Justice" in practice. I was honorably discharged while stationed in Kansas. I went to college in aeronautical engineering for three more years, when I finally began to mature. It was a slow shock: I am a self, not only my Mother's son, not a vocation, not only indulgence, I am me, and I here and now felt inauthentic. I dropped out of college and wandered, insecure but quietly self-content. Jobs were plentiful in the 50's.

> "Seeking" implies some sense of goal,
> wandering watches and hears
> without conceptual structure
> or creative focus. That same seed
> swollen, its crust a ragged shell
> annoying youth's brash foolishness
> but still hardened to greening sprout.

A memory. I could not go ashore in Piraeus, the seaport of Athens; a friend brought back two marble stones from the Acropolis, which I still have and feel close to, stones that many Greats had passed during enlightened Times, stones with vision and memories imbedded in their hardness. Somewhere between Eastern Italy and Piraeus I had a mystical experience…, but later I was less confident. Near our prior port of Taranto, Italy we had a Squadron Party, much booze and boxing, with a final game of tackle football. Everyone was banged up, bruised and bombed, most certainly me. Although I turned away from spiritual thought in those years, I was not ignorant of its quality. The peak experience as a realistic possibility informed my consciousness, lingering silently, like imagined memories in my marble stones: a peaked Presence silently looming but somehow isolated from mental form by hardened distance. Yet I can say with certainty that a degree of the "mystical" intensified my awareness of the Presence. I now knew Something did exist.

> Memories of sightless vision
> wither without effort's vector,
> resonance turned emotional
> distorts its Source. As a sunrise
> it briefly glowed, but to see what?
> > Possibility, like a seed
> > roots and sprouts by reaching out
> > for resonant nourishment
> > through kindred scents the mind has known,
> > we recognize and cultivate
> > only what in mind's soil's been sown.
> Possibility plants a need
> that directs personal effort
> to act towards probability
> scratching at an itching Presence,
> we gain more from what action earned,
> however feeble it might be
> than any "fact" believed or learned.
>
> In the Beginning is a means,
> there more important than its end,
> as a vague mystification;
> our means echoes our potential
> sounding from beyond mind-eye range.
> The rich scene a Way can present
> when enlarged by experience
> quickens and guides our resonance.

Spiritual resonance expands
physically and conceptually
as universal Unity;
its tone informs our structure's bones
deep enough to achieve: Something,
that might be done: Potentially.
Resonance is the quality
of the "mystic" experience:
the Cosmos is most often fused
for a mere second or two, then
weakens detuned very quickly
in memory's distorting eye.
The tone of Presence now lingers
within that consciousness, seeking
to recognize *It* formed elsewhere.
Full Enlightenment's Resonance
might best be represented by
the full harmony of Being
the Buddha attained and maintained
waiting, rhyming, calmly
beneath that Bodhi tree.

The "mystic" sensibility
often basks in complacency
justified by considering
the State as beyond mere reason,
it can become irrational
as professed in many fields
and taught by passionate preachers,
a proud blur of mindful Vision.

A Memory. My first job after dropping out of college was as an Inspector in the Thor and Nike Zeus Missile programs. I enrolled in a series of graduate night-school courses at UCLA in astrophysics, and finally found a field that could satisfy. One night during class the instructor took us to a large telescope and we viewed Jupiter and its moons. The sight was a Peak Moment in my life, those moons were completely natural, unforced, free, per Galileo not Newton; this I saw and this awareness I wandered with instead of astrophysics. That viewing was a spiritual experience, an access towards Something.

> My values since early boyhood
> existed, weak and unstructured;
> the Presence lingered, moaning low
> like wind through earned peaks, humming deep
> in concert with the green below.
> > *A moon's circular orbit is inertial;*
> > *its velocity vector is established*
> > *by its Source's size and mass.*
> Once touched and its deep pulse absorbed,
> Something lurked a concrete Presence.
>
> After years of haunting Something
> I knew the "mystic realm" *is,*
> widely inclusive, personal,
> much broader than sketched by scholars,
> more concrete than shaped by gurus,
> a quick flick of broad Resonance
> that can be returned to through mind,
> but turns dreamy as memory.
> Spirituality must act
> to vivify personally.

A sense of Presence, vaguely felt
before our subjective ego
poses in it as a framed mirror,
might be quietly actualized
by indwelling, by becoming
the form of its generative Source.
I indwelled the two-bodied State
as a simple Earth-Moon system.

Successful indwelling achieves
through unfocused Intensity;
belonging eventually seeps
bi-directionally, inward-
outward, vectored by firm patience
directing the mind towards knowing
as consciousness senses Being.

Interpretation can distort
the smell of truth
that brought thought there.
Words can lead as a molded scheme
but snub our gene of cosmic sense;
example: that insightful Truth
can at depths be irrational.

But the Real is not unnatural,
it's our curious mind probing
with imaginative daring,
that led us to the dark to see.
Eventually mind does correct
to rhyme, rhythm, and harmony
as consciousness extends us far
by glowing what we truly are,

> through Reason singing spirit's course
> evolved from our own uncaused Source:
> the omnipresent cosmos.
> But I soon learned that wandering
> does not a good employee make.
> I have said, mumbling to myself,
> I will not now accept any
> responsible job, my mind's stare
> is not there, spirit rhymes elsewhere.
> Working unfocused, mistakes lurk
> grinning behind a wall of dark,
> which lightened truth can circumvent
> in a blush of deep embarrassment.

After a series of jobs I found a rental situation that was ideal for my family, idyllic in its setting in Montecito, a suburb of Santa Barbara, CA. And within a few years I began managing its four houses, with artist's studio and storage structure and continued for over twenty two years. The only person that knew less about houses, etc. was the owner: an eccentric English Professor with a great sense of humor, which led (forced?) him to only seek (only find?) work in Arab countries in the Middle East. I managed that property while delivering mail at the Post Office.

> I live cherishing solitude
> knowing personal Resonance
> evolves from inclusive essence.
> I lingered there for years, content
> in its challenge, disappointed
> in my conceptual achievement.

A Note. The owner's second wife wanted to move onto the property with her father. I moved us to Oregon. Twenty years later the owner, his fourth wife and their daughter, along with that wife's son and his family, lived on the property, along with renters in the other two houses. All except the family's two wives, who happened to be elsewhere, died in the disastrous Montecito mudslide of January 2018, and all houses and structures, along with the property and two creeks, were totally demolished. A beautiful idyllic family memory, with a very tragic ending.

The only thing that interferes
with my learning is my education.

—Einstein

Science is a wonderful thing if one
does not have to earn one's living at it.

—Einstein

A Possible Means

"How can cosmic religious feeling be communicated from one person to another, if it can give rise to no definite notion of a God and no theology? In my view, it is the most important function of art and science to awaken this feeling and keep it alive in those who are receptive to it."

—Albert Einstein

In "My Introduction" I described my prolonged route during the creation of OR. I will suggest a related means within the same Way but more accessible and more readily achieved.

The Authority of my initial involvement was my Mother within the unique conditions of my childhood. The Source was the writings of China and India that she read to me. To a developed mind those writings are classic wisdom, but to me as a boy truth was there because my Mother said it was. Nevertheless it was actually there, and truth has a tendency to rise, adhere, and bond its source with a respectful sensibility. My route was long and inefficient, easily evaded by youth, but something real had been introduced in me, something I grew vaguely but increasingly aware of and which eventually created a Presence, humming inward and outward. Time spent with a vague Presence is itself an effective agent, just respectfully letting it sit and be, naturally intensifies and widens familiarity. An important factor in its development came about when I attempted to express some semblance of what my awareness sensed. However ineffective it was to others, it was my active involvement with truth, and this began a realization of my journey. The general method was to write whatever seemed significant then work my own thought, and all along the route any degree of insight or focus achieved was a very gratifying experience. This creative method wasn't a matter of merely refining words I had written, it was a means of penetrating and intensifying the clarity of my involvement with the real by slowly manifesting its Presence. I "did", I acted in that realm and achieved in my own. And once a degree of success through willful action is achieved, it readily expands as a need. Its Way now becomes more concrete and personal.

In OR the authority can be vaguely experienced in the general harmony of reason, which can intensify into a stronger more vivid Source as the unitive structure of the universe OR offers. Consciousness through awareness is the means of this Way, it creates a portal to the personal experience. The Form of the unity is created by a universal essence applying from the total universe as origin, and potentially extending more immediately as the relating world around us. This also can expand cosmically to suggest the all-inclusive unity that consciousness can slowly interiorize by sensing its own rhyme as Being within and as that Oneness. Need slowly develops and willful effort feeds the need; entities around us begin to be more widely recognized as manifestations of the essential State, and these can integrate to merge as a personal experience of the unitive resonance we and Reality are. This is the rational ground of the "mystic" experience. And I end this suggested means with the advice an ancient guru might have whispered to the receptive few stumbling along their Way, "Slowly, slowly, catchy monkey".

Poetry

The Hyphen

A human life will always trace
a dash that ends as tombstone date.
The name inscribed above that line,
meaningful to but a local few,
is a lifelong tag for a line too fine
to stand upon to view its Time.
The first date, warm with dependency,
cooled to personal wants; the last date
haunts every approaching moment
with echoes of prayer beseeching
beyond the cold doom of its fate.
Most histories beat with systoles
and diastoles that average to naught,
a thin bland line its times forgot.

But what if a hyphen offered a slit
through the wall of graffiti
our temporal abscissa seems scribed on,
presenting a view of there where
selves, belles, gurus, and infidels
resolve from and dissolve to,
we might then see from afar
what here and now we essentially are.
A life can become a vision with scope,
rather than righteously spent
lining caskets with hope.

Death cleanly marks extinction,
body and ego's nonexistence.

All in death, like a winter breath
diffuse in the cold cosmic mist;
only the living can see and be
the resonance of "eternity".
In our finite yet unique hour
rare eyes dare to stare
and work alone to hear and bare
the open sphere above and below
the clamps of their parentheses;
these lives fulfill the dates they bind
they see raw truth through form and rhyme.

While alive we can recognize
relational States near and far
as what we too in essence are.
We can this way address our State
mentally and creatively
extending being's true fusion
through poetic satisfaction.
    Never join in group graffiti
    it sears the brand of poverty.

Our hour can experience
what we all essentially are,
which continues when our life ends,
this is our personal Being
as the universal unity,
the terrestrial mirror
and celestial sphere
resolved in our immediate here
consciously, clearly, with reason
as its art, through science's means
extending rhyme through all States seen.

A life ends like a falling star,
a glowing scar ending in dark,
becoming a dimmed memory
clutched by a relational few;
a person can know of Being
only extended while living.
Happy Lifetime to you.

At a Mountain Meadow

Backpack to be in a meadow high
with enriching stream twisting
and frolicking like a playful child,
pausing at times to rest and sprawl
as a clear pool of darkened depth
with quick flicks of small hungry fish
catching the eye of passersby.
All around above the tree-line
ragged rock. From the trail can be seen
a Peak supreme, distant yet common,
aloof in ancient rhyme and space;
its higher crags smoothed in a glow of snow
above a mist of clinging clouds.
The Sun warms the scene towards clarity.

Pause with the meadow; listen
to its stream add trilling treble
to the canyon wind's basso tone,
both can fuse as a fugue of Nature
with heartbeat pulsing pleasing tempo.
That supreme peak centers the scene
with a sheen of white indifference.

At this height seek your Reality:
All's vague and confused near noisy crowds
but up here its themes flow clear.
To begin a Way is to see
A line of continuity

from grey myth to high glaciered stone
like sheets of tablet tossed askew
    ancient smoothed pages
    blank with torn edges
    asking your senses
    to see true the view.
The scope of reflection
extends on towards vision
when focused by knowledge
and entered through art.
Intensified immediacy
magnifies opportunity,
but a mind must be honed
for its own trek to start.

To continue is to sense self
out there in rhyming harmony
    reflective images
    mirroring the essence
exposing quite personally
    a spiritual nexus
    hinting formal context
a Way's course of consistency
where only belief could achieve.

Here can cherished solitude
bubble forth a creative flow
drawn down by Nature's gravity
guiding mind towards fertility,
where spiritual immanence
is free of impediments,
like a mute's prayer
in a silent Temple.

Roaming in the need of Being
stumbles along in clumsy steps,
without a firm sense of essence
daring can get lost, misspent:
even that great Peak
from its misted base
cannot a line of sight present.

Breathing the scent of shaded pine
that leveled to a bright meadow
blossoming an insistent Spring,
aching back and exhausted legs
sitting on stone, tired, alone,
can turn to its own inner ear
now set free by fatigue,
to hear the portal voice
of this revealing Way:
Welcome, Welcome, Welcome
each throb of pulse seems to say.

Where goes the light

Where goes the light
when the power's switched Off?
Where goes life's sight
when dark ignorance shrouds?
Where goes mind's rhyme
when its rhythms still cold.

Our defining state, relating,
persists beyond living sensate
   not as what it was
   but as what always is;
   not as ego orienting *me*
   but as life's tone of congruency
extending on as the unitive whole
in tune with all through essence.

For a mind alive to realize this
consistency as identity,
it must turn on the light
empowering mind's sight
to be the cosmic permanence
through knowing the real's resonance;
only living presents the state
of *eternity*, not empty death.
To not now stand and heed to this
will need to conjure perpetuance
bowed in the sanctity of dark.

A Prequel to My Introduction

Walking alone through clear old-growth
at home in their pillared temple,
where tree respects tree, relating
through safe distance, sharing Sun
    stunted growth encroaching their kin
    turn grey in their shade, unaware
    that Nature nurtures solitude
    as separation feeds green needs,
where a mind can hum alive with ease
like these tall trees in a high green breeze.

Tree hiss consecrates this silence
seeping deep in my fluid mind,
as I walk detached, it slowly
grows louder,
metamorphosing
into a slow River, a flow
down from a range of silent stone
on to the trees of green below.
The River brightens its forest,
like a source of liquid sunlight.

As I wander River widens,
and continues its expansion
into far mist fading the view.
The near bank beneath my feet leads
to a long line of spaced stones
stepping far out into the fog

       their separations seems no threat;
       their size, shape, and surface
       should not challenge balance,
I could not here but venture on
the need for seeking's momentum
feeds being's intensity best
through rare chances for rich new views.

The cold mist thickens through strange growth:
stout swamp trees wet with dangling moss,
their baseline thickened by strong roots
twisting hunger into the swamp,
straight trunks wrapped tight in clinging vines
binding together likened groups
while not extending to others;
dampened high in thickening leaves
unintelligible sounds
beyond seeing eye, straining ear
hears whisperings? hinting
of language phrasing?
Maybe not.
Odors strong in humidity
blend swamp bog with rotting debris.

Looking back, the stones I've traveled
vanish in mist; I'm abandoned;
isolated; my inner sense
loses its contact with my mind;
onward lies but a line
set in stone, its logic
pre-exists, obvious
but irrational, strange and blind,
advancement to be accomplished

through the placement of feet not mind
along its route of binding vine
shaping strongholds of their own kind.
No boat anywhere.

Water here is putrid, reeking
tense reptilian danger.
    Interpreting, analyzing,
      trying to make sense of a swamp
        slides the mind in thickened slim.
I stand here stranded on a rock
watching a patch of cosmic sky
often stating a soaring hawk.

I sit; detached in memories;
waiting; until the silent hum
seeps back, floating free submerged knowns:
    toned action will find direction,
    what I am will rise as equilibrium.
I now must swim to find the Sun.

So I swam and again I am
roaming alone like an unfinished poem
through a rich scene of reaching trees
that I through flow must make my own.
Like a River in a green forest.

Stages

Wolf crawled out of the den, away
from warm mate and playful cubs
to sit alone in the night, calm
and wide but now cautiously quiet.
His long howls to the Moon's Presence
spread a still far beyond its peril,
deep as that high night's eye, matching
its indifference, to then fall fused
in the dew of the subdued view.
In colorless moonlight
blending threat and beauty,
insects fear no wolf.

*

Rising in exhaustion, Alpha male
walked away from contentment, out
of his small band's cave, to sit cool
in his self with the night. Inside,
the group eating warm near the fire; here
a weaker but broader belonging, a Presence
sensed out there yet me, like looking
down to a pool of sky-water
or when dancing the Beast we feast,
or like a chill of unseen danger
when walking the night through looming trees:
    Some Thing is, here. A mental scent
    earthy yet rich. What? A kinship
    beaming warmth not threat. How? Who?

*

Extensive specialties bonded
our village. Wheat and barley
dried and stored, frees.
Irrigation planted us;
tended flocks pastured us
as does the Goddess we worship.
We exist quite comfortably
in Her beauty's fertility;
through duty we know unity.
    Gods will punish lust and greed;
        myths express what we trust and need.
    We commit, we share, we believe.
But then arrived the permanent freeze;
for lifetimes our soil was snow's cold crust.
we wandered, and settled, and wandered;
our just gods we just must trust.

*

Outside our polis, above a ravine
dwells the Oracle, a priestess hearing
the course of events in the wind
through the twisting oaks below.
But The Few turned away, to the Cosmos
from a nearer clearer deeper peak:
the mountain of formal knowledge.
Mind first sensed and successfully mimed
the Core Rhyme through music:
those key intervals long preferred in song
are clear ratios on the strings they sing from.
    The inner sphere is the outside's mirror

> their nexus hums of Unity.

Cosmic form, like our early speech
evolving since a milky coo,
was set in a natural music;
below its bonding form, balanced
deep within its structure, number:
ordered essence, consistency,
simple dynamic constancy.
> *The Presence rings out from a natural core*
> *reoccurrence will now imply much more.*

Rhythmic rhyme resounds most clearly
as the harmony of the Spheres, unheard
because our history's been deafened
by the beautiful affluence
of the solace of imagery.
> *The ancient Presence exists in our sense;*
> *the inner sings out when the outer's condensed.*

Geometry trains the creative mind;
abstraction deepens whatever eyes find;
science seeks order expressed through number;
philosophy enunciates clarity broader;
and art can the inner and outer combine.
We began eagerly,
sharing truth's pure beauty;
yet hubris, as "our *true greatness*"
defeated our society.

*

Reason had not spread wide enough
"to penetrate the Cosmic whole".
Yet the immanent Presence hummed
immediately, locally

beyond our intellectual grasp.
Some went alone seeking the glow,
some floated a portrait on-high
of those that sensed the world below.
Both means were early religion,
forming life's essence through ego
rather than ego through essence,
yearning for mystery
safe beyond learned reason;
and faiths sustaining a cherished belief
were easily lead by Priesthood through grief.

The richest gifts of earned vision
are focus and scope. Our science,
turning "counterintuitive"
through an extreme quantum context,
maintained focus but lost all scope;
spirituality has scope
but often blurs its own focus,
imposing scenes and Images
to better express vital truths.
Their redirected inner eye,
as if viewing through old stained glass,
sees naught beyond the message framed.

*

Our Times drift towards a cosmic Stage.
We the dissatisfied must blaze
a Way fusing mind and spirit
concretely and reasonably
to see beyond all Imagery,
raising awareness towards Being:

the self-inclusive unity
of rational Reality.
There we can belong, cosmicly.

More Concerning My Poetry

A poem is a sculpture in words,
a focused effort that can
animate a bland emptiness
by stimulating awareness.
Seeking poets strive to chip free
their own core concerns, shaping them
through vision, involvement, and need;
their labored refinements
polish our inner glow,
helping us extend
by reaching to find
more solid ground beneath our mind.

My poems, feeding need, stand and state
asking like minds to contemplate.
Spirit seeking focus through words,
seeing in scenes a quiet Presence
or sensing in Nature
its very own essence,
could view in stone a silent poem
as did young Michelangelo.

Reason heard, like a faithful's theme
can hum of deeper poetry,
its continuity mimes rhyme;
a fertile fact often transcends

its datum, extending harmony
as quiet mental resonance.
    Mind is the crucible
    that can still the ego
    to bare the spiritual,
a home where a poem can be born
formed warm within a family sense:
the womb of our intelligence.

Simple clarity vectors poems,
prodding a seeker's troubled mind
towards inspiration's downhill drive
by gliding on freed awareness.
Rhythm quickens and throbs its theme
like a native Indian dancing,
likeness adds scope to its tone,
rhyme at ends sings form through its scheme
inner rhyme brings immediacy home.
Its whole can chant the harmony
of inner-outer unity.

Truth deepens its depth in a poem,
Reality forms and moans low
through metaphor, and our spirit
strains out to Nature for echo.

A poem can vivify riches unseen
storing their value for others to find;
its nature then nurtures an ancient child
conceived through the union of spirit and mind.

A Triptych Night

(during a solo canoe trip)

A campfire casts an ancient muse
blending calm and mood with solitude,
becoming Nature's embryo
toned in warmth and crackling glow.
Ever since the haven of stone-age caves
flames entrance in their weightless dance
flickering this fuse of trees
quietly surrounding me
obscured by dark's immediacy;
staring at flames frees the mind
to rise towards quintessent emptiness
like the silent world lurking beyond
the darkened scene enclosing me;
as embers die, the vivid night
draws stars like some old memory.

*

My tent imposes geometry
where fear had ruled the ancient night;
stars bring light from their sacred heights
where gods had glared down power's decrees.
I sleep warm in our evolution.

*

River's easy flow rises high
at a large smooth rock , as am I
in the sight of a gliding hawk;
stilled leaves that began their form
in a dull tint of red
now twist green in a morning breeze;
seated on the trunk
of a fallen tree
listening to morning's soliloquy,
I swell in the warmth of cosmic Sun,
absorbing its sights that comfort me
as my cold hands embrace its warmth
through clutching my morning coffee.

Dragon

High in the rarified mountains
near the mouth of a comforting cave
lies a Dragon. Slumbering;
from time to time, raising a lid
to eye the world outside.

The cave hums busy contentment
toned in subtle shades of gray,
a sculpted shelter that is a home
for many different peoples. Peoples
are not my concern; but sometimes
at the lip, a Person appears
and sees in tune with grass and trees.
The Dragon then sneers flamed heat
and the person retreats,
the green vision reduced
to malformed memories.
The Person's turn is my concern.

This monster is not Fafner;
I'm no Siegfried; Notung
would cut through nothing:
dragons are not real. This is
some mental hologram,
a superposition of fearsome thoughts
projected from hallowed needs;
it's their interference, acting
constructively and destructively

that forms the spectral beast.
A stressful anticipation
generates the animation.

Yet its mien does kill
and its heat does maim;
it even stains the scene out here.
I bide quietly, out of range.
Human need has shaped that beast
and did so with authority.
I know its massive form is flab,
its bones structured by strong hungers;
W must regain core harmony
through working vague thought newly framed.
No one can kill that dragon,
it can only be dissolved;
and the acidic agent sought
must unify disparate thought.

Insight needs
truths of steel
propelled by zeal to penetrate,
then skilled will to decapitate;
so I stroll this springtime meadow
watching, learning, and reviewing.
The Dragon never smiles or frowns;
It's righteous, vicious, and quite proud
but neither does it roar or pursue.
I wait; I create; what more can I do.

Each vision seen
of reaching green
begins a branch in you and me

but needs our Sun's continuum
glowing the warmth of inner dawn
to continue bud and blossom.
I'll wait and continue, for now;
no more can I do, here, right now;

An Image for Reality

A god is a mirror not a lens.
Modern vision needs to heed
intimate congruency
within Reality, dilate
its eye to seek and try our mind's
logical probabilities,
not project our own self supreme;
the dangers of egocentricity
have long been a literary theme,
so let's move on.

Yet most good people need an Image
to draw out their spiritual sense.
I'll offer an alternative,
which could stir a scalar spirit.
This Image should be essential
to all life-forms, influential
in forming our terrestrial sphere
through sky and sea, the vehicle
and core of life, continuing
as sustenance for beast and tree,
a basic need of humanity.

*Let water be an image for
the nature of Reality.*

Colorless, odorless, flavorless:
to each sense merely a Presence,
by nature mysterious

in Nature ubiquitous
forceful in flow yet shapeless,
conforming to every vessel
while presenting in each
the shape of common ground.
A simple drink gracing thirst
can extend satisfaction inward
to feed a distorted need deep
beyond simple pleasure,
to then ease into blending calm.

We can sit with flower or tree
and fuse their sap through their beauty;
or push beyond aesthetic sense
by trekking with a group of friends
below high peaks of unseen end,
earning cool sweat on dusty aches
as pure personal achievement.
Our spiritual satisfaction
through any such participation
is like moving from city streets
to island shore, where we can dwell
in the pulse of healing waves, swell
with the breeze that seabirds soar
or like a dolphin, dive down deep
exploring schools and living things
like those around a coral reef.

Although water's free fluidity
can flow us beyond the nebulous,
a static pool can become a mirror
reflecting the myth of Narcissus.
We must move on.

Boyhood Memories

That pond* was near silenced tracks**
like those I tamped ties and lined rails on
in tenth grade, with gandy-dancers***
spitting tobacco juice
into our water tank,
causing pause in no one.

Walking balanced on rails extending
far further than the next slow curve,
underlines my boyhood.
I've often liked being alone
with guiding scenes reaching beyond
my sight, turning me more inward
towards something far, balanced, unknown.

Our backyard bordered railroad tracks
that lay ten to twelve feet lower,
rising to a long fenced field
more than two football fields wide.
There in summer pastured
neighborhood cows, that I
as a grade school boy, herded home,
each cow turning robotically
to be hitched in its own barn's niche.

---

*   the pond of "Basho's Frog", another poem, was about a half mile further East than "that field", along the same railroad tracks
**   these tracks were now no longer used, the iron mines they served were closed
***   this was our name for permanent track-gang workers

Another poignant memory
is returning home in dark on
that same field, a moon-sheened
unity of crusted snow,
from a hushed day with naked trees
   in northern Minnesota winter,
   looking at trampled tracks and scat
   around a lean-to I had built
   sheltering bread crusts, corn and grain.
The buoyant world of powdered snow,
dried by severe cold and wind-smoothed,
swirled and whipped at every lift of drift.
The sky cleared deep to vivid stars
long before suppertime;
my village spreading points of light
without height, failed its cosmic mime.
I owned snowshoes, rawhide and wood
nearly as tall as me, each step lifting
a load of dry snow, making walking
heated labor, a condition
keenly respected, exertion
quickly draws exhaustion
suggesting sleep, which will
effortlessly and peacefully kill.
Even as a young boy
I was informed by this,
it had occurred locally.
The weight of death so near
sank deep but bore no fear.

That covered field was my youth's muse.
I would often stop, to rest, letting wind

cool my neck and chest; I then could view
the field I knew. Meadowlarks sang
below the snow, their aural scene
now silenced white, submerged
like a transcendent truth
lurking in a ground of green;
the winter wind droned
its quiet freeze in monotone.
My fugal remembrances end
as lighter themes of floating s birds
unseen above my homeward herd.

I can still sense them, echoed
in rivers and clouds and trees:
formative scenes of memory
enhancing my immediacy
as I walk the balance of Nature
while seeing and Being alone.

Wolves

Two days canoeing and camping
before I awakened to see
the Boundary Waters Wilderness
as not just a stretch of islanded lakes
with hills and shores of evergreen
without cabins or cars
invading the scene,
but as primeval purity preserved
in the severity of noble indifference.

To a canoeist, an optimal world;
a sanctum fused with Canada
north of Ely Minnesota,
Sigurd Olson country, a favorite
of both sons' boyhood reading.
No motors allowed to foul the sound
no structures or scars of power lines,
even planes must pass by noiseless high;
this was the ground that trees had graced
when glaciers warmed, where caribou herds
had flowed in peace past Ojibway wigwams.
A land of boyhood memories
setting my life's prime similes.

Later I opened spiritually, beyond
the bind of a viewing mind;
I was here free of debris,

exposed in raw immediacy,
not through some biased myth like *Hiawatha*
set in a Song of meager promotion,
but with rock turned green
in this floating scene,
evolution's quite sacred devotion.

Essential form floats like shadow
    through a growth of parallel pine,
      like the innate state Cezanne had shown
    like the echoing rings in tree and stone
blending the quiet indifference.

Paddling through spray of wind-torn crests
towards where we wanted to be
means turning to meet waves reinforced
more directly, yet acutely,
engaging the challenging thrusts of nature;
paddling through ripples of sun-tipped breeze
to explore some bay or continue on course
frees focus to turn to the ease of our speed
through tempo's flow, rather than force.
Paddling can rise to spiritual heights,
gliding rhythmic efficiency
towards a rhyming congruency
with planets in orbit and hawks in flight.

    Mid-May, white-capped and cold
    dawned with a spring
    to sunburn calm.

We made another day-excursion
stretching the route beyond our plan,
ending with a muddy portage

into Thunder Lake. There, wolf tracks,
scat with fur. Many prints, different sizes
most quite perfect, as if purposely placed.
We camped nearby; that night
we heard the pack across the lake.
The dark was clear, the half-moon
strong and cold; a dull sunset, void
of clouds had dimmed to a vivid dusk.
Playful loons had turned mournful;
the clean quietude stilled inward
tuning tonic themes to minor moods.
We watched the night, without wanting,
silent, each in solitude, eldest son and I.
We heard the wolves again, much later
moving northwest and distant.
Both events were short
but permanent; the pack was
young yapping and chanting adults.
We listened in a glow, watching
the strange dance of campfire flames.

> An sacred scene, searing deep
> a resonance sympathetic
> with the moonlit leaves
> of my backyard tree.

I slowly labor my awareness
into vision lensed by words;
the wolf howls.
I pulse belonging into poems
but often fail; the wolf succeeds
and any poet would know it.

The perilous harmony of the wild
with chords deep in our dissonant times,
is best expressed by the wolf.
Its summer howl knows winter storm
the whirling snows obstructing its needs,
then with long interval leaps, slides free
to the warm den of family: committed
to exhausting hunts of dangerous prey
and nurturing cubs with frivolous play.
Experts say the reason wolfs howl
is to proclaim territory. I hear
the wolf resounding Being's fuse,
a state extending night's deep glowing;
the wolf howls as nature's muse
and, endangered
sends its poem up with foreboding.

The wolf lifts skyward nature's hymn
whispered by wind through noble pines,
its message thins dim yet potent and true
supported by rock, echoed in blue;
this poem exulting such involvement
engaging minds enriched through rhyme,
offers its memories in reverent homage
thanking the wolf for moments sublime,
enshrining the wolf in the soul of Our Time.

Seeking a Taoist Gate

via the Cascade Mountains
(but finding it closed)[****]

As thrusts of pulse in late blue sky
each peak uniquely similar,
no mist, no floating clouds, no snow
just mountains of cold clarity;
ancient rock, firm above
columns of mountain fir,
pillars that could lift troubled minds
upward through their Temple stillness,
a timeless scene, natural beauty
enchanting the eye, and thereby
sealing my spirit's exclusion.

I wait in distorted shadow
cast by a lone pine
into a pile of rocks
that seem to mimc the larger scene;
mind reaches, as I extend
slowly with patience earned,
knowing how I've learned to blend,
like that tree shadow, an arrow

[****] in homage of the many Chinese mountain hermits that sought their Buddha nature by living alone in thatch-roofed stone huts for years, freeing their mind through meditation, daily Taoist or Buddhist services, their daily chores, and Nature.

dimly leaning Eastward towards
a sky empty yet a Presence,
tree's vectored shape fusing fulfilled
in deeper shade from westward forms
slowly spreading their darkened flow
rising upward towards peaks tinted
in alpine-glow. I watch, I wait…
colors fade in dark's monotone

> *rock peaks, diminished by distance,*
> *near pine alive, reaching towards stars*

suddenly a low pitched bird-trill
ignites a swell of immanence
dense with essential eminence,
a portal opens,
                  to flow
the quick of unified scene
blending with the still in me.

Femininity

Baby's empty stare suddenly
widens aware, recognizing
the softened mound of hungry warmth.
Mom dawns in a first focused smile.

Kindred belonging, realized
deep and personal, is sustained
in a Mom's femininity,
natural grace with intensity
in a lyrically toned presence
that can lean forward tenderness
from a core of sincerity
as mankind's nearest form of beauty.

Every young man becomes aware
of the feminine,
watching it slowly maturing
difference into difference
expanding in vulnerable charm
shaped in a swelling form
rising to sexual attraction:
a tsunami wave flooding mind
diluting but not dissolving
the completing person she is.

To the agèd male, accepting
sexual involvement has faded
in like lives, femininity

can stream her own life's home, from eyes
of awareness with natural sense
now secure in experience.
We elderly can lay embraced
sharing smooth curves of softened skin,
cherishing total naturalness
with rich familiar moments
through the grace of face and lips,
nipples and organs, that slowly
resolve the longer we lay
to inner calm and belonging.

That bond is worldwide, transcending
huts and homes, beliefs and cultures,
extending on to some degree
in each lifeform's nesting family;
humans can expand this further
as our spirituality
focusing sensibility
towards universal unity
with all of Nature,
                                which began
through a strain in swollen pain
from the warm dome of womb,
into Mom's loving smile
as the hearth of a home.

The Cave

Gathered about a peak like darkened mist
thoughts slowly coagulate
without shape yet stilling action
like a snapped twig in forest dark
or the trill of an unseen meadowlark.
I take the moment to The Cave

to settle in calm quietude
with patient anticipation;
I am comfortable here. The Cave
is now my home within our home,
yet often accompanies me
like a haunting memory.
Here silence muffles outside noise
with dark echoing resonance
sympathetic with my own;
here, immediately,
is where I feed my need
here can nurture Being.

Peaks rise spiritual in Sunlight,
our Cave, from resonance we've earned.
Formed rhyme can free a clinging thought
to seek like roots on naked rock
a fertile place, a sunlit plot
to grow and bring the birds to sing.

Truth blends best in quiet dark;
we are the Sun, we are the lark.

A Quantum Function

A young frog sits on a log in a swamp
croaking in June 'neath a nonlocal moon,
but his tune turns refracted
by passion's thick tension
towards a very cute frogess
floating stilled in suspension.
Contiguity is no factor here,
clearly it's "entangled separation"
that stirs this quantum State of Relation.
  "I see the moon, the moon sees me,
  we both see you peeking
  'round that bayou tree",
posing there with those long firm legs....
Let's collapse our wave function's
mere probability, appear
at a tangled locality
and send forth quanta
of pollywog eggs.

Here is Where

Here is where I want to be;
I'm rooted. My large yard
I know quite intimately:
tending tends to extend
but I do not pamper,
green too needs freedom.
Why would I want elsewhere
when here I can be me.
I do travel, appreciate
view and rejuvenate, I feel
I might root most anywhere, maybe
even deeper, thicker maybe,
but why try. Greening takes time.
Only reaching roots can earn power
only firm stems can bear their flower.

I attend by pruning the old
and planting both color and food;
my poems grow the ancient anew
casting seed midst a hungry few;
it's the green fields of eager minds
that groom the bloom of fertile times.
Immediacy forms my territory;
here is where I need to be.

Words Without Art

> My words fly up, my thoughts remain below,
> Words without thought never to heaven go.
>
> —The King, in "Hamlet"

Bold hypotheses structured logically
without our spirit's bonding poetry,
placed the stars far beyond Our Time
severing us from source and rhyme.

Our eye's ear is detuned today
we conjure where we use to say,
but mind's and spirit's concert "A"
always was and always will be
Nature's simple harmony.

When thought floats up,
and sense remains below,
the thought never rings a cosmic echo.

Cross-Country Skiing

Our trail was spoiled by olden snow.
Crusted by days of melt and freeze, fouled
by debris dropped from the trees, it dulled
our youth's efforts by collapsing
under each forward step, sinking
deep into sweating exhaustion.
Lower down the effortless slope
were well-marked trails, each scribed tale
related yet unique, all scrolled
skillfully when stating their mode
as our sacred yellow-brick road.
No spiritual truth could youth earn;
we could but watch, listen, and learn.
Numbed by fanciful speech and pose
we sensed the mind's lament unfold
deep within our structural bones.

As we aged, clean snow fell
thickened and slow, slanting
from an Eastern flow towards
our vision's need for truth
to blaze a natural Way, a muse
rhyming Source with personal course.

Then youth's obstructed embryo
released to sire a vivid Sun.
We now ski along, each alone,
sharing the strain of breaking trail,

looking outward to see inward,
finding shapes on blank waves of white,
twiggy lines of extended shade
outlining brightened emptiness.
Bare trees, like insights rise upward
towards high white echoes floating smooth
within a view of clear blue Sun
fronting the unseen constant dark
that binds this cosmic scene as One.

To know the flow of cross-country skiing
on the contoured glaze of the Sun,
can smile with the glide of planets;
our focused exertion spurs on
latent needs seeking expression,
as our clouded breath gasps spiritual rhyme
that mimes the fusion within with the whole.

Tree

I think that I shall never see
a film or photo of a tree's
reality. Its beauty, maybe
but how to show that balancing need
up from the ground's deep servicing
on to the sphere it feeds and cleans
while drawn to the Sun's rich energy.
Each brown reach extends its green:
a State of Relation
as rivulets that soar
a calm yet eager form of flow
sent skyward to embrace the whole.
The mind can know what the eye can't see,
but only Art can present a Tree.

Harness the Beast

Never ride the tail of a beast;
harness that strength, put it to work
this could lead you to
where you want to be.
If you arrive at The Lake
give her drink and a washing,
move that Mom to the shade
but always swim alone;
beasts will only muddy the pond.

You can float like a cloud in The Lake.

Ageing

Firmless muscle loosely aligns
the grind of worn joints, bone-on-bone,
good eye squints as ear leans in close;
mind, vexed by misted memory
freezes in silence, embarrassed
by stubborn name or wandered date;
sleep is stayed awake by loud thought,
walking is cautiously awkward
no longer corrected by quick,
yet all of ageing's crippling flaws
draw us to the Immediate.

Our sentence of immediacy
limits the reach of roaming eye
while widening sense awareness,
not of current events or crimes
or "us vs them" rotting Our Times,
instead routing mind to the real:
the vague Presence in the present
of a tone blending near and far
the natural chord all lifeforms are.

Now, set the sensed Immediate
within a mindful consciousness
involved as an essential State
by thickening and quickening,
rhyming by reaching out its core,
sensing being in local forms

all evolved from the uncaused Source,
distant yet here within our sight,
most vivid in the dark of night.

Age can ache Being's poetry
focused in Immediacy.